Please enjoy!
Nancy Corzine
2009

NANCY CORZINE
GLAMOUR AT HOME

BY NANCY CORZINE
WITH ROBERT JANJIGIAN

BOOK DESIGN BY DOUG TURSHEN

RIZZOLI
NEW YORK

Dedication

It seems only proper that I would dedicate this book to the three people who made my life as rich as it is today: my mother, my greatest champion, who believed and convinced me that I could do anything; my father, who in his quiet and ever-direct Scandinavian way, inspired my work ethic and taught me the importance of honesty; and my wonderful Harold Stern, who loved and believed in me without reservation, and who made me believe in my talent.

And to my grandchildren, I leave this legacy, a chronicle of my work, to remind them of the beauty in the world and life's possibilities.

Coco and Lily, the "girls," are a constant source of joy in my life. Here, they perch on the Florentine, a favorite chair.

Contents

Introduction

My father and mother, Ralph and Rita Johnson, with me at the beginning. *Previous page:* A comfortable seating area is part of a Hamptons master-bedroom suite. *Following page:* The still-life composition on a pair of walnut cocktail tables in a Manhattan apartment includes Murano glass candlesticks, a mid-century alabaster vase, and a piece of natural coral mounted on an acrylic base.

There was once a little girl who wanted to be a fashion designer. Though she lived in Seattle, far from Paris, Manhattan, or Hollywood, places where elegant and beautiful women could be seen wearing the latest haute couture gowns, she had dreams of creating her own designs. She would eagerly await the latest issues of movie and fashion magazines, clipping pictures of her favorite stars and models in all their stylish glory, making scrapbooks with the images. She was obsessed with the idea of beauty and glamour. The little girl's parents were creative in their own ways. Her father was an expert woodworker who could build just about anything. Her mother was a weaver and an accomplished seamstress. She made the little girl's clothes and taught her to sew well enough to make frocks for her dolls. Not an athlete, the little girl was thus encouraged to turn her attention to creative pursuits. She loved to stay home and keep house. The little girl's father made her a dollhouse, which kept her busy for hours every day. She would never tire of rearranging the rooms to suit the life of their make-believe occupants. Her father once told her something she'd never forget: "I don't care what you do in life, just do it better than anyone else." Her mother always encouraged her, saying, "If you can think of it, you can do it." That little girl is me.

From the beginning, I grew up with an appreciation for the finer aspects of life. I have always had a curiosity about well-designed things, whether they are clothes, automobiles, chairs, or homes. My father's love of wood was passed down to me. My mother's appreciation for textiles and love of gardening and entertaining has been a part of me from the time I was asked to help her in the kitchen and set the dinner table with silver, china, crystal, and flowers. I wasn't always so interested in gardening, but I know that now, later in life, it is her influence that has brought me to appreciate the beauty of the outdoors. My mother was also an intrepid collector who took me along to flea markets and antiques shops all the time.

I believe there was something inside me from the time I was a child that spurred me to follow the path toward a career in interior design. I don't think my experience is unique, as over the years I have met many others like me, who were in a similar place during their childhood. Whether we grew up in modest or wealthy circumstances, we eventually gravitated to design and developed into professionals. Over time, while working our way up as I did, we knew early on that we were destined to create more beautiful environments. As we played with our dolls and made scrapbooks of our favorite rooms and houses, we were practicing our future craft. While playing with my dolls in their dollhouse, I initially fantasized that someday I would make my mark in the fashion business. However, looking back on it, the dollhouse was where I was most comfortable.

I started my design career working on what I now look back on as clean, pretty bare-bones, functional commercial interiors for a Seattle office furniture company. I eventually left my hometown of Seattle to go to Los Angeles. I had wanted to live in Los Angeles since my first visit to California, at six years old. California was truly glamorous, beautiful, and most importantly, sunny—especially for a girl who had grown up in the rainy Pacific Northwest. As I gained more professional experience, I learned a great deal about construction and architecture. I also supplemented my on-the-job training by reading everything I could get my hands on about design and architecture, following the work of some of the legendary designers of the twentieth century. A few years later, I decided to focus my attention on the design and manufacturing of furniture. I started with a small showroom at the wrong end of Robertson Boulevard, the traditional center of L.A.'s design community. I did this with the help of my mentor and friend, Harold Stern.

A single call from the great hospitality designer Louis Catalfo, who proposed that my firm supply furniture for the new Century Plaza Tower Hotel that was being built in West Los Angeles, was really the start of what has grown to become the Nancy Corzine company. With this first big job, I was faced with the task of making furniture in quantities that I was not equipped to handle. I was a hands-on person then, as I am decades later, determined to learn how to make the best furniture possible, without sacrificing quality or appearance. This is what led me to opening my own factory. It was not as easy as it sounds, and there were many challenging and humorous situations that lead to the success of our factory. However, things turned out well, and led to more projects, primarily from the hospitality design industry. To meet the demand, additional production facilities were acquired, and we expanded our factory to finishing and upholstery.

In the late 1980s, my focus returned to the residential side of the industry. Our company expanded its range of product offerings to include furniture for every room in the house, along with fabrics, lighting, and accessories. We worked hard to establish a national presence for the brand and opened showrooms across the country. The look I have refined, which I call "transitional," combines elements that are classics of every era. The original piece may be an eighteenth-century French antique or a mid-twentieth-century American or European design, but what makes it successful and desirable, even glamorous, is its translation as a comfortable, practical, and useful addition to an updated interior.

Design is not just my passion; it is my life. I was once told by a very wise person that it is ideal when one's work is also what makes one happy. In my case I consider it not only ideal, but truly a gift that I am able to follow my dreams in an industry that I am so passionate about.

Initial Impressions

Entryways

If there is something I have learned, it is that the first impressions you make will not be forgotten. From the sound of your voice over the telephone to your appearance to the look and feel of your home, the memories will always remain.

Whether your entryway is a soaring, double-height foyer with a beautiful staircase or a modest, less dramatic space, some attempt should be made to set the stage for what follows. The glamour quotient is heightened when, at first glance, there is a distinguishable tone. It may not be apparent when a person initially steps into the space, but as he or she moves about the home, even the least design-aware should recall how it all worked together from the beginning.

The design style that I have developed and continue to refine over time requires a degree of discipline, a confident eye, and a commitment to the creation of integrated and consistent spaces throughout a home. The aesthetic standard is established in the entryway. Though it may be a transitional space, only to be passed through momentarily, the statement it makes should be memorable.

As a designer, I am known for mixing modern and traditional-style furnishings with antique and vintage pieces. My taste generally leans toward contemporary design. I am not a fan of the overstated.

But, the decoration of the foyer should be looked upon as a place where exceptional, unexpected statements can be made. A particularly stunning painting or a strategically positioned piece of furniture can be the most effective means of setting the tone. So, too, a beautifully carved mirror, an unusual or oversize chandelier, a collection of photographs, or a dramatic sculpture will make the space striking.

There are several practical considerations for an entryway. Any of the following elements can add beauty as well as functionality: A coat closet or other designated spot where visitors may easily leave their outerwear upon arrival is essential. Either will ensure that the bed in the guest bedroom remains unscathed. An umbrella stand is not only useful; it can also serve as a wonderful decorative piece. There are many options available—everything from porcelain to leather. I personally prefer antique porcelain, as it tends to work with many different design styles. Not only does a console or chest add interest, it can also accommodate a variety of essentials. A glistening silver bowl on top of a console makes a great place for those keys that tend to get misplaced. It can also function as the spot to deposit the daily mail or newspaper. If space allows, a magnificent table in the center of the foyer makes an elegant focal point and pedestal for floral displays. There is no amount of art or furniture that can replace flowers arranged simply. Not only do they add great warmth, they also can be used to reflect the season.

The entryway should suit its surrounding environment, whether the home is a city apartment or a country house. A clear indication of the locale should be obvious upon opening the door. This does not, however, mean to say that there cannot be an element of surprise. Entry points are not just front doorways. The experience of a house can change at every turn of a corridor, at the top of a stairway, or at the approach to another level. The key aspect is the visual enticement of the visitor. The goal is to tell a style story from start to finish.

A sculpted, curved stairway is the opening statement made in a Palm Beach town house that has been completely remodeled to appear more open, spacious, and unmistakably luxurious.

Above: A third-floor landing in a Los Angeles residence featuring a series of photographs of geisha is accented by a Ming dynasty chair. *Right*: Matching chests in a dark, walnut finish are placed on either side of a kitchen doorway in the gallery-style foyer of a midtown Manhattan apartment. Photographs of Venice and Paris by Alexey Titarenko add a romantic touch. A large painted and perforated canvas by Anne-Karin Furunes introduces a mysterious quality to the space.

In the double-height entryway of a Hamptons residence, a selection of antique pieces, including an eighteenth-century Aubusson tapestry, a nineteenth-century French refectory table, a circa-1780 Gustavian long-case clock, and a circa-1880 hand-painted papier-mâché jardiniere, set the stage for a traditionally inspired design. The recently built home was devised to have the appearance of a centuries-old shingle-style manor house.

Left: At the end of a central passage that provides access to several rooms, a mirrored niche was created for the display of a late eighteenth-century Portuguese porcelain stove. *Above:* At the end of an upstairs hallway, a pair of hand-painted chinoiserie-style panels offers the look of a mounted folding screen, but they are in fact doors to a linen closet that serves adjacent bedrooms.

Above: A second-level landing features a round antique Italian country table and a selection of elements from a variety of places and periods. *Right:* A glimpse of the entrance to the master suite is afforded through the doorway. In this transition space, a series of framed prints backs up a vignette composed of English and continental antique furniture and objects.

Choosing Lighting

aturally light and sunny spaces are my preference. However, when the evening hours approach, it is important to ensure an adequate, balanced level of artificial light. Dimmers are essential to control the lighting
effect you desire and deem appropriate for the moment. They also allow for variance when you want to set
a particular mood, especially when you are entertaining guests for the evening.

I have always loved Murano glass. There is something fascinating about it, its Venetian heritage, and the expertise required to fabricate each beautiful piece. My appreciation of its artisan quality is reflective of my artistic side. Murano
lamps and chandeliers are especially effective when positioned in contrast to heavier geometric pieces. Carved, wooden
table lamps with metal-leaf finishes are also particular favorites of mine, as are strong, sculpted bases of any material.
Again, it is the juxtaposition of materials that adds interest when a lamp is placed on a table, desk, or bureau with a differing
texture. And certainly large-scale chandeliers used in foyers and dining rooms provide a wonderful sense of drama.

I prefer designs that have a strong, substantial presence to those that are more delicate. Make sure, however, never to
install light fixtures or lamps that overwhelm—or underwhelm—the other elements in the room. While mixing period
fixtures with more contemporary light sources can work, it is often a safer bet, especially when a room has original architectural details, to locate authentic pieces that are in keeping with the age and style of the house.

An appropriate shade is an important part of a lamp. I prefer plain linen, silk, or lacquered varieties. Scale and proportion are the most crucial considerations in choosing the correct shade. With lamps and fixtures, it is all about scale and
about finding elements that work in harmony to create a more finished environment.

In the entryway to a Palm Beach high-rise apartment, a pair of bamboo
candlestick lamps in a Venetian-sterling finish has been placed atop
a highly polished *demilune* chest. The Murano glass mirror, centered
above it, reflects the vista beyond the main room of the residence.

Whether constructed of wood, metal, or glass, a table lamp, floor lamp, or chandelier should have a strong silhouette. These designs reflect a range of influences—from sleek mid-twentieth-century modern to interpretations of classic Murano glass creations by Seguso to traditional carved-wood styles.

Vibrant Spaces

The Living Room

Before designing any room, it is important to consider its purpose: how the space will be used and what role it plays in the life of the house or the apartment. When I am invited into someone's home, either as a guest or in a professional capacity, and see that the living room is a relative no-man's-land without an ounce of personality, I find myself thinking, what a shame. An inherently practical person, I believe that a room should be used to its best advantage. Traditionally the most generously scaled room in a home, the living room should be comfortable yet gracious, and also reflect the personality and lifestyle of the residents.

A principal room in most residences, the living room should be an attractive and inviting environment in which to be. It is also the most public space in a dwelling, where visitors are taken first and residents pass through or by on a regular basis. This is especially important to remember when dealing with a more modestly sized home, where there may be limited areas for relaxing, reading, entertaining, or just sitting down by yourself to watch television. When this is the case, then the room cannot be treated like a field that lies fallow until the next family gathering or holiday party.

If there is another common space, such as a family or media room, a den, or a library, so that the living room doesn't by necessity have to be a multipurpose room, then it still should not be presented in an untouchable, precious, or uncomfortable fashion. Even the most unused living room shouldn't look unlived in. A living room should never be so formal, so spare, or so sumptuously fussy that one hesitates to enter it. I always recommend keeping the decorating scheme clean and relatively simple, even when integrating antiques, art, and traditional and contemporary furnishings and accessories. In an overly decorated room, the hope for any semblance of graciousness being communicated goes right out the overly dressed window.

Regardless of the dimensions of the space you're working with, you should try to create at least one conversation area. More than one is ideal—if you've got the space. There is nothing worse than the inappropriate positioning of a chair out of the sight lines of others in the room, in which somebody may feel slighted or isolated. One of the reasons sectional sofas are such a successful part of many living-room scenarios is that they create instant and natural conversation areas.

Upholstery and wall colors are most attractive when they "glow" by day and have a soft, romantic appearance by night. My preference is for golden tones, neutrals, and whites, and for a lighter palette altogether. Avoid muddy or drab tones, which tend to steal any semblance of "lift" from a room. When selecting fabrics, always be mindful of their ultimate use. A beautiful silk taffeta may make lovely window treatments, but it is not suitable for heavily used sofas or sectionals. For these items, a chenille or velvet is ideal. On the same note, when considering the finish for a furniture piece, keep in mind both usage and appearance. While a painted finish on a carved chest of drawers enhances its detail, the same treatment looks lifeless when applied to a flat surface.

Collections of rare and fragile accessories should be treated with care and kept out of harm's way. A beautiful cabinet with glass doors or a bookcase, appropriately placed, is ideal for displaying those special objects that give warmth and add interest to any room. When combined, all of these elements make for an interesting living room.

Right: In a grand Park Avenue penthouse, one section of the window-lined living room features an elegant seating group, with a mid-twentieth-century–inspired sectional sofa covered in silk velvet and two mid-twentieth-century–style slipper chairs surrounding a generously scaled Venetian silver-finished cocktail table.
Following page: When designing a living room, no matter what its proportions, it is important to create separate but related conversation areas.

A sectional sofa was chosen as the most interesting solution, both visually and practically, for the corner of a Manhattan high-rise living room. The large-scale cocktail table serves many purposes and is especially useful for casual buffet suppers.

Left: Lightscape, an L.E.D. work by Leo Villareal, is a focal point in a living room, where a collection of contemporary art is displayed. The seating group adjacent to Villareal's work includes a vintage Dunbar cane-back chair and an armless sofa. *Above:* Another large-scale artwork, *Grasses*, an oil painting by Antonio Murado, hangs on the wall in the same living room.

Brazilian cherry wide-plank floors provide the perfect dark base for a thoroughly white-walled Los Angeles living room, where a seating area is furnished simply with a sofa, chinoiserie-style coffee table, and vintage mid-twentieth-century chair. The area rug is Chinese wild silk.

Above: In a Los Angeles living room, an acrylic table is placed beside a vintage stainless-steel–based chaise covered in ivory leather. *Right:* The etched-bronze cocktail table is by Philip and Kelvin Laverne. Cane-back Edward Wormley chairs, designed for Dunbar in the 1960s, complement the clean lines of the sofa.

Left: It is all in the mix, with a high ceiling and dramatic backdrop. This Los Angeles living room features a sectional sofa as well as pairs of cocktail tables and "social" chairs, complemented by a photographic composition by Elizabeth Gill Lui. A collection of blue and green Murano glass pieces is displayed in a mirrored, shelved niche. *Above:* In the Los Angeles house, an intimate place to lounge, adjacent to the dining room, is perfect for predinner conversations. Custom-built banquettes flank a pair of sterling-silver–leafed cocktail tables, and a buffet accented with Murano lamps and a sterling-silver–finished mirror completes the setting.

In a vintage Palm Beach living room, a traditional Gustavian-era look is achieved with mostly new elements that reflect an array of period design inspirations. The existing paneling is whitewashed, and pale-blue fabrics have been introduced to create a soothing ambience.

In a Palm Beach high-rise apartment by the ocean, the sectional sofa in the combination living-and-dining room is positioned to take advantage of the spectacular vista.

A range of light-colored shapes and elements, related to the oceanfront location of the Palm Beach apartment, has been selected for the living room, including a pair of "social" chairs, a sterling-silver–finished cocktail table, a mirrored accent table, and a silver-finished side table. The sectional sofa is covered in velvet, with pillows in a linen-velvet–patterned fabric.

A pale, monochromatic palette works well in small-scale rooms, such as this Miami living room. A maximum amount of comfortable seating is provided without overcrowding the space.

Above and right: An acrylic cocktail table contributes to the creation of a sense of spaciousness. When not in use for dining, a collection of Chinese porcelains is displayed on the marble-top table positioned in the entryway. *Following pages:* A blue-and-white theme was the client's only request for the design of this country house in the Hamptons. The furniture arrangement in the living room is ideal for casual entertaining and balanced without seeming contrived. An Alexander Calder lithograph, hung above the fireplace, adds a spark of color.

Sectionals are ideal for tight spaces, as in this Miami house. Keeping wall decorations minimal and large in scale helps to make the room less cluttered in appearance. A chest, providing needed out-of-sight storage, serves as an end table.

Cool tones and light-reactive elements and finishes are brought together in a Southampton living room, where a limited palette and subtle introductions of pattern and texture make for an ultra-sophisticated statement. The framed photograph is by Rosemarie Laing. The sculpture is by Stephan Balkenhol.

The living room of a Los Angeles penthouse features spectacular double-height ceilings. A number of vertical elements have been incorporated or created to highlight the generous height. Bookcases line one wall of the space, which also includes a dining area. Asian, African, and European art and artifacts contribute visual interest and warm up the room significantly.

A spectacular antique Coromandel screen is a singularly dramatic element in the Los Angeles penthouse living room. The mixture of a sea-grass carpet, a contemporary bronze cocktail table, a large-scale sofa upholstered in English linen, and continental antique accents makes for an interesting composition.

Above: Tablescapes that are well edited add warmth and personality to a living room space and reflect the individual interests of the residents. *Right:* A collection of books integrated into a living-room scheme, especially when there is no other place to display it, adds another layer of depth to the space.

Choosing Fabrics

The first fabric collection that I ever put together, when bright and flowery chintzes were all the rage, went against trend. While working with an Italian mill, I decided to design a new collection inspired by historic documents that I rescaled and had woven in linen in a contemporary style. To add to the mill owner's distress, I chose to color my designs in soft and pale shades, instead of in traditional jewel tones, and to make the repeats oversize. The mill owner did not believe the collection would sell. However, he was proven to be incorrect, as it became one of my firm's most popular. I have never veered from this basic aesthetic path when it comes to color, design approach, or fabric selection.

My favorite fabrics are neutrals. I find that neutral colors are the most soothing to introduce into a room, as well as the most practical and timeless. (Along with them, I recommend painting walls in paler shades or in white, both of which lend a luxurious spaciousness to a room.) Within a space, I generally employ mostly solids and quiet patterns, some with interesting monochromatic textures or subtle variations in tone.

For dressing windows, similar fabrics are desirable. The intention is never to hide the architecture of the room or to inhibit the stream of light coming through a window with overly ornamental curtains or draperies, but rather to enhance the elegant simplicity and dimensions of the space. Light-reactive fabrics, such as satins, taffetas, and anything with metallic threads incorporated, are a means of bringing shimmer to the equation. If a spark of color is something you cannot live without, choose a complementary tone and introduce it sparingly. Fabrics selected for the home should never be so fragile or delicate that there is constant concern about their upkeep or replacement. Antique or vintage fabrics, tapestries, and embroidered textiles should only be used on pillows or accent pieces.

A pillow covered with a hand-beaded chinoiserie-style fabric and edged in silk fringe lends glamour and interest to any sofa.

In a sweepingly scaled
Hamptons living
room, dual seating
groups are established
by the positioning
of sofas back-to-back.
An antique console,
on which a pair
of Italian ceramic
balustrade lamps has
been placed, bridges
the two areas.

Seating areas should be designed for comfortable conversation and easy access, as well as to be used for afternoon tea, cocktails, or buffet-style suppers. In this Hamptons living room, antiques are mixed with contemporary pieces, and a generously scaled cocktail table is a focal point. An armoire to the left of the fireplace contains a television that is easily accessible but hidden from view when not in use.

A chinoiserie-style secretary works as a display case and functional element in the Hamptons living room. This magnificent piece holds a collection of antique leather-bound books, an antique tortoiseshell tea caddy, and a French bronze Napoleon III clock.

A corner of the living room is enriched by custom-designed bookcases with glass doors and light, decorative molding work, where collections of antique books and seashells are displayed.

Living With Art

Works of art should be part of every room. Though I do not consider myself a serious collector, I have purchased art for many years. I introduce paintings, prints, photographs, and sculptures of all shapes and sizes into my own homes and have been called upon by clients to assist them in selecting and incorporating works of art into theirs. You should acquire a particular piece because you love it. If you are considering the purchase of an artwork merely because of its provenance or potential for return on investment, or because everybody else you know likes the artist's work, then you should probably pass. I like a mixture of period and modern furniture, accessories, and art. The use of contemporary art should not be restricted to rooms that are designed in a contemporary style. Nor do spaces that have a traditional or period feel require traditional art or art of the same period.

In placing art, it is important to consider the relationship between the work and the scale and proportions of the room. A large wall requires a large-scale piece. An intimate space demands something smaller. Art needs room to breathe. I choose vibrant pieces for neutral-toned rooms to introduce color. I also find that works of art with a graphic or architectural presence provide effective contrast. I prefer to display works of art in a gallery style, making sure that pieces are hung or displayed at the proper height and appropriately lit so that each one is shown to its best advantage.

A monochromatic palette allows for works of art to be the focal point of a room. The color and texture of an oil painting by Antonio Murado brings warmth to a Palm Beach town-house living room. The custom sectional and large Venetian silver-and-marble cocktail table create a dramatic setting.

The color scheme in this contemporary living room is primarily neutral, with color and accents provided by a series of large-scale botanical prints. A chrome pendant lamp and a collection of mercury-glass accessories add sparkle to the space.

The backdrop to a simple, symmetrical living-room seating area, contemporary shell prints, framed in a variety of styles, have strong visual impact. The sofa, covered in linen damask, a Venetian silver glass-topped cocktail table, and a pair of armchairs with linen slipcovers make for an inviting and attractive grouping.

Choosing a Sofa

There are hundreds of styles of sofas to consider when designing a room. I have found that tuxedo-style sofas or sectionals, or variations of them, are the most useful and work well in a range of schemes, including those with a mix of antique and contemporary pieces. These clean-lined sofas look best and offer the most comfort and versatility when the back cushions are loose.

There are many other traditional and contemporary options available: elegant camelback, rolled-arm chesterfield or club, low-arm Bridgewater or Lawson, sleek mid-twentieth-century modern, as well as variations on all of these classic shapes.

A sofa is an essential element in living and other sitting rooms and should be chosen for its individual appeal, comfort level, and intended purpose as it relates to a particular setting. Keep in mind that in most conversation groups, no more than two people will likely sit on a sofa at any given time. Even for large gatherings, longer models are usually not the best choice, either aesthetically or from the perspective of personal comfort. When selecting a sofa, consider the style, scale, and fabric that will best complement your room.

The glamour of mid-twentieth-century Hollywood style is captured in this living-room scenario. The hand-painted tea-leaf silver screen evokes a sense of glamour and light. The clean lines of the blue linen-covered sofa and the cream-colored lacquered tables add to the crisp look. An armless lounge chair and circular rosewood cocktail table complete the setting.

A sofa anchors any conversation group, but it should also stand alone as a useful and sculptural presence. These sofa styles are derived from traditional as well as modern designs, and any one of them may be combined with other pieces to make a fresh, eclectic statement.

Rooms for Entertaining

Dining Spaces

A beautiful dining room is a delightful present to your guests. It is the one room in the home that constantly may be reinvented to suit the occasion. The fantasy begins with the choices of china, crystal, linens, and flowers, all of which are used to create a memorable table. When setting your table, remember to think outside of the box. Never be afraid to mix different patterns and periods. Use silver or crystal pieces that may be intended for other purposes. A soup tureen can function as the base for a wonderful centerpiece when filled with flowers or fruit, and porcelain figurines make great holders for place cards.

Selecting the right dining table determines the style from which a great dining room begins. A pedestal table, particularly when it's in an oval shape, allows you the flexibility to accommodate several more chairs. After you have selected a table, it is the appropriate time to consider wall backgrounds. I personally love chinoiserie-style paper and find that it works with any look—traditional or contemporary. Other options include lacquered walls, grass cloth, and faux finishes. Don't forget the ceiling. Silver tea paper applied above creates a wonderful, reflective glow.

The dining chairs are the single most important design element in the room. I prefer to have the chairs stand on their own—that is, not to match the table. There are a number of things to consider when selecting chairs. Comfort being paramount, not all chairs are created equally. Make sure to test-drive them first. Always keep in mind that cramped quarters never make for a gracious setting. You want your guests to have an enjoyable dining experience. To accomplish this, the size of the chairs is important. Don't be afraid to mix not only styles but also chair sizes and upholstery fabrics. When accommodating additional guests, smaller wood-framed or upholstered chairs around the table add interest.

In my mind, the ideal dining room table seats as many as twelve guests. As mentioned previously, a pedestal table and a mix of chair sizes will allow for larger parties. For more intimate dining rooms, the same principles, scaled down, can be applied. No matter what the size of your space, there are certain ingredients required to create a wonderful environment. Experience has taught me that in addition to a table and seating, a serving surface is helpful. It could be in the form of a console or even a shelf if the space does not allow for a more generously scaled piece. A sideboard or buffet, however, with drawers and doors, is always the best choice as it provides a place to store items used for setting your table. I always recommend choosing one with a marble top. It is always convenient to have your linens, silverware, and serving pieces close at hand.

Another important aspect is the lighting. The traditional choice is a single chandelier above the center of the table. Depending on its style and size, this type of fixture may not allow for the placement of candelabras or large centerpieces on the dining table. If candlesticks or grand flower arrangements are favored, then use surface-mounted fixtures or recessed lighting. Wall sconces make a great addition when placed around the room or on either side of a mirror or artwork. And, of course, candlelight creates a glamorous ambience that no other form of light can achieve.

Right: This open Los Angeles dining room offers flexibility and has a definite sense of spaciousness, under a vintage Tommi Parzinger chandelier. The clean-lined traditional walnut dining table is complemented by mid-century-style side chairs covered in warm-toned, textured silk velvet. *Following pages:* In a Manhattan dining room, *Ice Scapes*, an oil painting by Antonio Murado, provides a dramatic background. A highly polished rosewood pedestal table allows for ease of chair arrangement, with a vintage Murano glass-and-brass chandelier centered overhead. Windows have been left untreated so the high-floor view can be enjoyed by day or night.

This Palm Beach dining
room has a clean and
contemporary feel. A wall
covered in mirrorwork reflects
the garden outside. Iran
Issa-Khan's photograph
Monstera Deliciosa is
a bold addition to the space,
adding drama and interest.
The room is anchored by a
rosewood-and-acrylic table.

Originally enclosed, this room in a Palm Beach town house has been opened up to both the living room and the outdoors, and converted to an intimate dining area. A glass-top table with a silver base and leather chairs were chosen for comfort and their contemporary look. Punch-art photographs by Vik Muniz add color and provide contrast to the white walls and marble floors.

Left: An acrylic table and vintage Edward Wormley cane-back armchairs are positioned for a bird's-eye view of midtown skyscrapers through the floor-to-ceiling windows in the corner of a Manhattan high-rise apartment. The elegant gilded-bronze floor lamp is a mid-twentieth-century French piece. The glass collection is Murano. *Above:* A Palm Beach breakfast room, papered in warm grass cloth, is simply furnished with a modern-classic Eero Saarinen tulip table and chairs under a Scandinavian artichoke fixture. Framed photographs by Evelyn Lauder add a color-rich accent to the background.

A traditional hand-painted silk chinoiserie design has been used to paper the walls in a Hamptons dining room that has been set up with a mixed group of chairs around a double-pedestal table. The English Regency–period sunburst mirror adds brilliant sparkle to the space. The chandelier is carved wood with a silver-leaf finish.

Above: The beautiful finish of this walnut burl table is not lost, even when it is set for an elegant meal with a variety of elements collected over the years. A mixture of antique linens, silver, and china adds interest. *Right:* An étagère in the dining room is the perfect spot for a display of Paris porcelains dating from the eighteenth and early nineteenth centuries.

Chairs and tables not part of a matching set are the most interesting choice when designing
a sophisticated dining room. In this room, which is separated from the living area by a fireplace,
painted and stenciled cane-back Louis XVI chairs with linen cushions share the space with
a walnut Regency dining table. The Italian chandelier is finished in sterling silver.

Choosing a Dining Chair

I love chairs. In fact, the first piece of furniture I ever designed was a chair, though not of the dining variety. My modified and updated Directoire style–influenced design has been a best seller in my collection for years, due to its versatility and elegant proportions. In chair design, it is not just the look of the chair that should influence your decision, but more importantly how comfortable it is, which is achieved through proper pitch and support. If anything is off and a chair is uncomfortable, you will know it immediately upon sitting down.

A dining chair should always be the best and most comfortable seat in the house. Before addressing issues of style, there are some practical considerations to keep in mind in selecting the right chair for your table: The height of the seat should always be in scale to the height of the table. Generally, chairs used for dining should have seats that are eighteen-inches to twenty-inches high. Typically, dining chairs are designed to fit under tables that are twenty-nine to thirty-one inches high. Approximately twelve inches is the ideal space between the surface of the table and the surface of the seat. This amount of space will accommodate most people in a comfortable fashion for an extended period of time.

Once a chair is deemed comfortable enough, then the choice of style comes into play. This process involves the positive evaluation of the chair's functionality in combination with its aesthetic value. For visual variety in any space, but especially in the dining room, I avidly endorse the concept of "mixing it up" in terms of periods and styles. There is no need to go with a matching set, even around the table. It is much more interesting to include eighteenth-century French, nineteenth-century English, Swedish Gustavian, mid-twentieth-century American, and European chair styles in the same room. The aim is to create a different, somewhat more eclectic, and slightly more unusual effect.

Stylistic mixes are more intriguing to the eye, as in this dining room. A heavily carved and painted French dining table is combined with lacquered Chinese Chippendale chairs on an Oriental carpet.

Classic and contemporary
reproductions of chairs from
a variety of historical periods
are a more practical option
than antique styles, as they are
the proper scale and height,
as well as comfortable.
Whatever the design—sleek and
modern, or more formal and
traditional—a chair should
complement the table and add
interest to the composition.

Place Settings

Whether for a relaxed meal served family style in the kitchen or for an elegant dinner party in the evening, a simple table setting is my recommendation. The atmosphere you create should be beautiful, with a touch of fantasy or drama, yet you must not forget that the point of any gathering is to encourage lively conversation around the table. While the presentation and enjoyment of the cuisine is important, you never want anyone to feel intimidated by the formality of the service or the preciousness of the tablescape. A festive and attractive table should always be your goal, but keep in mind that a table set with restraint and a classic sense of placement and proportion is generally most effective.

As someone who has a deep appreciation for the beauty and luster of fine woods, I do not often use a tablecloth. I prefer linen place mats to designate each dining position at the table, with the rich tabletop exposed between each place. Choosing the china, silver, and linens is an aspect of having a luncheon or dinner party that I relish. Making a handsome and inviting table, even for the most casual of meals, makes for a more enjoyable experience.

A vase or bowl of fresh flowers is always a lovely addition. However, make sure to select stems that are not too tall. There is nothing worse than an arrangement that blocks the view across the table, inhibiting eye contact between those seated opposite one another. Flowers should not be too fragrant. Though scented candles are lovely sensory accompaniments to most rooms of the house, they are out of place in the dining room.

In terms of seating, I prefer, whenever possible, to mix it up by putting people who have never been introduced next to one another. It makes the experience all the more interesting and lively. I have always loved to have dinner parties where guests feel they have met someone new—and maybe even made a friend for life.

Right: Fresh flowers, beautiful silver and china, fine linens, and flattering light make for a gracious and inviting setting for enjoying delicious food and pleasant conversation at the dining room table. *Following page:* Two mixed arrangements of ranunculus, calla lilies, orchids, and roses brighten up a dinner-party setting in a Los Angeles residence. Seasonal apple blossom branches in Murano glass apothecary vases add drama. The candelabrum is a coveted Tommi Parzinger piece.

Left: An informal and intimate supper is served on cocktail tables with a silver-leaf finish in a Los Angeles home. Colorful crystal and simple arrangements make for a festive, yet casual atmosphere. *Above:* The use of place cards, even for smaller dinner parties, adds a sense of specialness to the occasion. The contemporary crystal is from Bulgari.

Flowers add vibrancy, interest, and color to the dining table. Centerpieces should be simple and low so as not to hinder the view across the table. Arrangements for other areas can be taller and bring a sense of the season to the interior. Mixing china patterns and glassware makes the table setting and meal all the more memorable. Linen place mats and napkins, antique or new, provide an elegant background for the china, crystal, and silver.

Above: If there is not the luxury of such an extra space, a handsome cart or console, topped with a silver tray and crystal decanters, may be substituted. *Right:* A bar area, carved out of an unused closet, can be a jewel box. The installation of mirrored walls and a mirrored ceiling, along with glass shelves bring glamour to this newfound space. Beautiful crystal heightens the bar's sparkling appearance.

Working Retreats
Libraries and Offices

A house seems empty to me without the presence of books. I am an avid collector of all kinds of printed matter; and for me, design, fashion, and art books, both contemporary and historically oriented, are indispensible when I pursue new furniture and fabric designs. I like to have inspirational reference tools on hand, to page through on a regular basis, and to share my particular passions with friends and clients. Books of all types, depending on individual interests ranging from current novels to literary classics to lavish art monographs, add warmth and interest to any room and point to a level of cultural curiosity. The books that people collect tell me more about them than any single element in their home or office.

Many people do not have room to spare for a designated personal library. However, books don't have to be displayed in a single space; I consider them an essential element in nearly every room of the house. Built-in bookshelves can, and should be, installed in the living room, dining room, kitchen (especially for cookbooks), bedroom, and multipurpose den or family room. Arrange the books with decorative objects, framed photographs, and even small paintings. The most pleasing displays are tidy and focused. Books don't have to be relegated to shelves. A stack of novels and biographies by the bedside always feels right to me as I usually am reading several books at the same time. Positioning books on a cocktail or end table may be cliché, but I love having them there, where they are available for flipping through at will. A space that is used as a library does not have to be just about the storage and display of books. Though, of course, a comfortable place to sit and the installation of good lighting are essentials.

When setting up a home, the room that I refer to as the library may also serve as a dining room, a den, or a home office, with all the necessary electronic elements incorporated within its parameters. In a pinch, it might even serve as a guest bedroom, with the right choice of furnishings, such as a daybed or a sleep sofa. This space can also make a great additional gathering spot, one that is comfortably furnished in a similar fashion to what might be included in a more formal living room, with all the same components arranged in a scaled-down, slightly more casual fashion.

I am constantly at work. That is just my nature. But I also like to have a separate work area at home, something I have found that clients also appreciate in their residences. It may be the library or study, or even a corner of a bedroom, but some kind of fully equipped work zone is necessary. When devising a work space, remember that the idea of appearing organized and businesslike does not preclude a sense of design. In the offices I put together, I strive to create an environment that reflects my approach to residential living spaces and that is in tune with individual aesthetic preferences. Comfort; multiple places to interact; interesting as well as useful pieces, such as a vintage cabinet or a one-of-a-kind desk or chair; and professional polish are the key elements. Most people will spend more hours of the day in an office than in any other place, so the decorating scheme should be geared toward making their time there pleasant and attractive, as well as be impressive and glamorous to those who pay a visit. Comfortable seating and an area for less formal interactions, such as a living-room–style arrangement, if space allows, are ideal.

As someone in the design business, I've come to realize that my offices, whether at home, in my factory, or in my showrooms, are indeed my calling cards, reflective of the style that I have made synonymous with my company's image. The business that I established caters to a discerning group of interior designers. The overall look I convey to these aesthetically aware professionals must demonstrate a certain sophistication and casual elegance.

A place to work should be designed with efficiency in mind. A view outside, with natural light, is always preferable. This leather-top walnut desk has a curve to it and contrasts with the selected chair and its sterling-silver–leaf finish. Additional light and interest is provided by a vintage Murano table lamp.

In a Los Angeles home, a bedroom converted for use as a study serves several functions. It is a private place to work, read, watch television, or even nap. Prized photographs by Jacques-Henri Lartigue are positioned on one wall that has been given architectural interest with a gridded series of applied moldings. The etched-bronze cocktail and side tables are by Philip and Kelvin Laverne.

The library of this Hamptons home is designed for a range of activities, including watching television, reading or reflecting by the fireplace, enjoying a cocktail, or playing a game. A fine watercolor landscape is displayed over the mantel. The walnut cocktail table has an antique tooled-leather top.

SWIMMING POOLS

ART + ARCHITECTURE

A game table and antique French bridge chairs occupy a corner of the library by the fireplace. The bookshelves hold a variety of current and classic reading materials as well as a collection of early twentieth-century French hat forms.

The traditional wood-paneled library has been sleekly updated in a Los Angeles house. The space is also used as a media room, with a built-in large-screen television and a place to play games or have a casual supper.

A pair of vintage French, leather lounge chairs with ottomans is at the center of the media room. An antique Ming chair has been added for interest. A large floor mirror reflects a view of the bookshelves, while serving visually to expand the space.

Vintage black-and-white photographs of director Alfred Hitchcock and actress
Marilyn Monroe were chosen for the media room, which includes a bar counter.
The etched-metal table is a vintage design by Philip and Kelvin Laverne.

The glamorous Harry Benson photographs of stylish guests at Truman
Capote's 1966 Black and White Ball are
positioned behind Nancy Corzine's
desk in her Los Angeles office. Her
custom rosewood desk and credenza
are dramatic yet functional.

Workspaces, no matter how generous, should have a residential feel to them, if possible. Custom walnut bookcases line the wall of Nancy Corzine's Los Angeles office. The seating area, a place for informal business discussions, features a sectional sofa, a pair of hammered-metal-and-sterling-silver cocktail tables, along with a pair of vintage tub chairs. A Jean-Henri Jansen tiger-maple cabinet with chinoiserie-style paneled doors is a striking addition to the office scheme.

The office in a
Manhattan apartment
is organized for comfort
and convenience, with
a table used as a desk
and a credenza for
always-needed storage.
Artwork enlivens the
work environment,
along with a contempo-
rary lamp with a silver-
leaf shade, which is
also a necessity. The
framed black-and-white
photograph is by Jeff
Reese. The photograph
of a horse printed
on aluminum is by
Charlotte Dumas.

Homework

An allotted space to work at home is something I consider critical. Others seem to agree with me, as I am asked to incorporate home offices into many residential projects. I have been convinced over the years, as I have added work spaces to my own houses, that it is a great luxury to be able to work from home in a pleasant, separate room that is also a well-appointed office. It is both convenient and time efficient to steal a few hours in the evening or on the weekend to catch up with work.

The home office, whether it is tucked away in the corner of the bedroom, the kitchen, or the living room, or located away from the main house, is an extension of the residence. Designing a space primarily for work does not mean forgoing attractiveness. The arrangement of strictly practical rooms should reflect the same approach taken in planning any other interior space. I find it convenient to have open shelving, where all reference materials, books, files, and tools are accessible and neatly organized. If you have meetings at home, there should be ample seating, so that everyone is comfortable. A proper work surface is essential. The traditional choice is a desk with storage, but a good-looking table can work just as well, as long as there is storage elsewhere. Good lighting is vital in any work space. Although a computer, printer, fax machine, and other equipment are necessary in a well-functioning office, they should be hidden, if possible, with all wiring concealed. An attractive cabinet or chest chosen for this purpose is most desirable to keep the office clean, uncluttered, and attractive. Whatever the size or location of your home office, it is an important and well-used space that deserves as much attention as any other room in your home.

In Nancy Corzine's Hamptons home office, French shelving provides storage for baskets and books. An antique English partners desk serves as a generous work surface.

Above: The rear wall of Nancy Corzine's home office is mirrored to reflect the surrounding garden. *Right:* No matter what the season, the light-filled exercise room adjacent to the workspace feels as if it is outdoors.

Private Retreats

Bedrooms and Bathrooms

To my mind, a place to sleep, perchance to dream, should be designated as a sanctuary. This innately romantic room, where softness is a hallmark, should exude a feeling of tranquility. The bedroom should be your personal space and a place where you can escape from the world. To relax, to steal a few precious moments of restful seclusion . . . that is my idea of heaven.

When envisioning a bedroom, I not only consider comfort but also privacy. I picture the room as an enclave that is self-contained. Be it for a bit of work, a short nap, or catching up on a little reading, a bedroom ought to be an environment where you are able to accomplish many things in peace. It should have the overall effect of a secluded living room, though on a much smaller scale. When possible, I like to include a desk and a seating area. But the greatest luxury of all is a fireplace. I love to lie in a bed and read while enjoying the warm glow of a flickering fire.

The single most important component of the room is the bed, which sets the design. Whether it is a black chinoiserie-style four-poster bed or a simple headboard with a clean line, your bed should always be an expression of your personality. The choices of bed linens and comfy pillows heighten the experience. Other important elements are small bedside tables or chests for either side of the bed. These should be beautiful as well as functional, and, depending on personal needs, there are a number of other requirements. Drawers are perfect for housing remote controls, a pencil and a pad of paper, a flashlight, or eyeglasses if you need them. I find it convenient to have good bedside lamps, preferably ones with dimmers. Always remember that it is important to create an environment that is enticing. I make it a habit to provide guests with the same comforts that I enjoy.

With bathrooms, I prefer to think in "spa mode," even if the space is small. A deep, inviting tub is something I can't live without. There is no better sleeping pill than a warm bubble bath. A great shower, with multiple heads, adds to a spa-like feeling. When space is not an issue, I convert a chest or dresser into a vanity cabinet. It affords you plenty of cabinetry for the storage of life's accoutrements, and the result is more interesting. Double sinks, especially in a bathroom shared by couples, are a necessity. Many heated discussions begin over whiskers left in a porcelain sink or toothpaste smeared on a marble countertop. Mirrors in the bathroom not only are functional, they also can have tremendous impact and add glamour. They make a small area appear much larger, as well as provide additional light.

A closet or large-scale dressing room, either of which is an essential element of any bedroom plan, is a space where practical touches are necessary. When planning the layout of the closet, remember to install good lighting, something that is often overlooked. I like to use washable wallpaper in closets. This application adds a more finished look and alleviates the necessity of repainting often. Worth its weight in gold, an organized closet can save much frustration and valuable time. There should be a great deal of thought given to its design. Getting dressed is so much easier if everything is in its place. A stool, or a bench, and a stepladder are always useful to have on hand. Maintaining the same decorative scheme throughout the bedroom, bathroom, and closet or dressing room creates the effect of a luxurious suite.

Right: A soothing environment, rendered in calming, restful tones, was the goal in the design of a Palm Beach master-bedroom suite. Contemporary shapes and a delicate antique Swedish bench work in tandem to create an interesting interior. *Following page:* What better choice than a mirrored four-poster bed for a high-rise apartment master bedroom with dazzling views of the New York skyline? A Marc Chagall lithograph hangs over the bed. Acrylic bedside tables with vintage French bronze-and-crystal lamps add to the glamour quotient.

In the Manhattan master bedroom, the luxury factor is evident with the introduction of a blend
of comfortable yet rare elements: a 1940s Andre Arbus desk, a delicately carved bergère
in a Venetian silver finish, and an acrylic side table, all reflected in a large, mirrored screen.

The master bedroom of a Hamptons country house is designed to be a comfortable retreat for enjoyment during the daytime and evening hours. The room is dressed in a pale parchment color, with a single silk *matelassé* fabric throughout. The rug, a Tabriz, adds color and interest to the space. The antique youth bed, placed at the foot of the master bed, is a finishing touch that is attractive and is now the home for the family's two Yorkshire terriers.

A fireplace and seating
area in a master-
bedroom suite makes
it more luxurious and
enjoyable, as well
as more comfortable.
In this Hamptons
bedroom, the painting
over the hearth is
an eighteenth-century
French interior study.
The andirons are
unique nineteenth-
century French designs.
An unusual antique
French chair adds
interest to the room.

A coordinated wood-rich look was achieved in a Los Angeles master bedroom, by hanging a pair of Jeff Reese photographs above the headboard and positioning a leather-upholstered bench at the foot of the bed. Bedside tables were ordered in different sizes to fit the space. Classic swing-arm lamps provide convenient reading light and free up space on the bedside tables for family photographs and other necessities.

The spacious master bedroom allows for a substantial seating area, created with a pair of black lacquer Tommi Parzinger daybeds upholstered in rich hand-blocked silk Venetian velvet. The round, etched-metal coffee table is by Philip and Kelvin Lavern. A series of black-and-white portraits of Hollywood icons is displayed. The room, with its elegantly curved perimeter wall, features a fireplace and ample space for a handsome vintage desk.

Headboards are a must, but they need not be conventional or made originally for this purpose. An antique Chinese screen works well in a Hamptons bedroom, mixed with pieces inspired by French and English traditions. Plaid silk draperies soften the expanse of windows. The French chinoiserie-style bedside table dates from the eighteenth century.

A custom vanity cabinet, in a black-crackle finish with chinoiserie-style hand-painted decoration and a marble top, adds a substantial look and plenty of storage.

The Best for Guests

When hosting friends overnight or for a weekend, I want to make each one feel comfortable in my home. I strive to create guest rooms that are fully equipped and set up to make their guests feel welcome and relaxed. My early career experience, working alongside some of the most talented and innovative luxury hospitality designers, taught me several things about creating the perfect guest-room experience. This knowledge, combined with what I have learned over the years from being a guest in some of the finest homes, has influenced the way I approach putting together a guest room.

Anticipating basic needs, such as sleeping comfort, adequate storage and lighting, and privacy, is only the first step. A desk or table, if there is room, especially for those who may have to mix business with pleasure, and a place to sit other than on the bed, are also preferred elements. Whenever a suite-style arrangement is possible, with a separate seating area for lounging or taking an afternoon doze, it makes for more comfortable guest quarters. Having a current selection of magazines and books on a variety of subjects on hand, a television, and bedside tables supplied with drinking water, notepaper, and writing implements, further serves as a signal that guests are welcome. Ample closets, with room to store luggage out of sight and plenty of hangers, are a necessity in gracious hosting.

Each guest bathroom should be stocked with a generous supply of fluffy towels, a robe, grooming products, and a hair dryer. I also like to welcome guests with arrangements of fresh flowers in their rooms. It is thoughtful touch—and one that shows you care.

A New York City apartment guest bedroom offers all the comforts of home in a simple, yet luxurious package. The gouache above the walnut leather-upholstered headboard is by Alexander Calder.

A guest bedroom is a place where sumptuous comforts should be provided, along with all the necessities. Stools placed at the foot of the bed offer a visual break from the luxurious bed, while complementary bedside chests provide always-needed storage space.

In this Southampton bedroom, a blue-and-white palette has been effectively embraced, but in a subtle, soothing, and appropriate fashion. A lounge chair and ottoman provide a comfortable place for reading and relaxation.

A guest suite created in the style of a private apartment is a rare pleasure that guests will enjoy. The sun-filled bedroom of a Hamptons home features all the necessary elements—places to sleep, work, and relax. A table desk and chest are used as bedside surfaces. The room includes a mix of traditional and contemporary furnishings and finishes.

A toile de Jouy fabric sets the style tone in a Hamptons guest bedroom. The combination of furnishings and finishes from the mid-twentieth century and Biedermeier period makes for an interesting look that is carried through to the guest bathroom.

Choosing a Bed

The central element in the bedroom, the bed, should appear neat, inviting, and perfectly in tune with its surroundings. Comfort is the first priority. When purchasing a box spring and mattress, I make a point of trying them out first and comparing the levels of support. What is considered firm for one person may prove to be agony for another.

The choices of bed linens and pillows are of the utmost importance. The pillows you select can make all the difference between a restful night's sleep and a fitful one. The decision between the use of a comforter or a blanket is principally guided by personal preference, but the weight and warmth of the covering should be determined by the climate or the preferred temperature readings in homes where air-conditioning or heaters are seasonally in use.

The style of the bed, be it a four-poster bed or just a headboard, determines the design of the room. Your choice may be traditional or contemporary in style, but it should always be a reflection of your personal taste. The size of the room will dictate the scale of the bed. It is important to allow space for other necessary furnishings.

Comfort and convenience, with a certain amount of airiness, are key in designing a wonderful bedroom setting.

Whether contemporary or traditional, architectural or fanciful, the style of the bed—which should be a beautiful object on its own—sets the tone for any bedroom. Beds with art deco, English, French, and Scandinavian roots can be used as the base from which to build a bedroom scheme.

Mirror Image

I am always in search of interesting and unusual mid-twentieth-century and antique furnishings. Some I add to my personal collection. Others I employ as models for fresh additions to my furniture or lighting lines. Years ago, while on one of my periodic expeditions to flea markets and antiques shops, I came across a beat-up, poor-quality chest sheathed in mirror. The extremely delicate and broken-down piece, which I scooped up immediately and set to restoring, struck me as a special find. This single object inspired what has become a signature of mine—the many mirrored bureaus, cabinets, tables, desks, bathroom vanity cabinets, even beds, that I have designed and installed in numerous homes. While mirrored pieces, which are innately interesting, romantic, and reflective, have become increasingly popular over the years, they have always been a favorite of mine for the light quality they naturally bring to any space.

The introduction of mirrored furniture, a mirror-covered wall, strategically placed mirrored screens, and framed mirrors either hung on a wall or leaning against it, can improve the look of an ill-proportioned or tight space. Mirrored walls are best when they reflect a view of some kind, expanding the visual horizons of a room and bringing in more light. A well-placed wall of mirrors can give the impression that the room is twice the size it is. Mirrors can be enlisted to bring the outdoors in and to brighten up a space, especially a light-deficient one where the addition of a window is not possible. My preference is for clear mirrorwork—over antique, distressed, or smoked glass—for its clean, cool, sleek, and contemporary appearance.

A mirrored chest is converted to an elegant vanity cabinet in a windowless Manhattan powder room that has been brightened with a tea-leaf silver wall covering. Crystal drops on silver sconces, along with an antique Venetian mirror, take the glamour factor to another level.

Above: A mirrored vanity with a French-style stool with a silver-leaf finish makes a glamorous and feminine statement in a Hamptons master bathroom. Regency-style lamps are hand carved and finished in Venetian silver. *Right:* The walls of a powder room in a Hamptons residence are covered in a Thai pinstripe silk and adorned with a series of silver-framed antique botanicals. Lighting is provided by French bronze sconces dating from the 1920s and an English chinoiserie-style lantern overhead.

Glamorous master bathrooms, such as these spaces in Palm Beach, *above,* and Los Angeles, *right,* appear even more elegant because of extensive mirrorwork. The looks created in these rooms are sleek and sophisticated.

The Hub

Kitchens and Storage

The kitchen is the most utilized room in the home. It is designed for two main purposes: cooking and serving. Part of the entertaining area, it should be as attractive and comfortable as the rest of the residence. I believe in creating a place to gather in kitchens, as it seems inevitable that guests are drawn to this room. It is the informal hub of a home and should not be overlooked in terms of aesthetics. There should be a place to sit, even if it is just a stool or two pulled up to a counter. Because casual family-style meals served in the kitchen are a favorite of mine, I try to incorporate a table and seating in every kitchen that can accommodate them. My favorite arrangement is a pedestal table with a banquette and additional chairs.

Experience has taught me that the layout of the kitchen is important to its success. I follow a basic design structure that has proven to be invaluable: I think in terms of a triangle when determining the placement of the sink, the cooking area, and the refrigerator. Without fail, this layout helps to facilitate a natural, balanced work flow.

Plenty of open counter space is preferable, as is the addition of a center island. If you're a cook, or you live with one, you will find that extra surface space is always welcome. Countertops should add to the visual appeal. In recent years, I have grown fond of using man-made stone, which is impervious to stains, marring, and chipping, while providing a pristine appearance. I suggest incorporating the same material as a backsplash for added sleekness. In smaller, darker spaces, it is a good idea to install a mirrored backsplash to lighten up and extend the space. Under-counter lighting also opens up the space while providing needed task lighting.

When you go to the trouble of making this workhorse of a room appear visually enticing, everything should have its appropriate place. The kitchen cabinets should reflect the design and style of the rest of the house. My preference is for simple, white or light-colored cabinets. Clutter in general, and unused objects and appliances sitting on the counter collecting dust, are unattractive. There are many well-designed appliances available on the market. When selecting kitchen equipment, keep in mind the look of the room and how it will integrate, and be stored, within the overall space.

When entertaining is a regular event in the household, it is a smart move to double up on the essential, larger appliances to create an efficient and user-friendly environment. If accommodating multiple cooks or a catering staff, you may want to consider the addition of a second refrigerator and dishwasher, dual sinks, and perhaps even a second oven or expanded stove top. A wine refrigerator and an independent icemaker are also helpful.

I prefer to use a single flooring material throughout all rooms of a home, including the kitchen. A better visual flow is achieved in the space when the flooring remains consistent throughout. Though decorative floor tiles are often the first thought for kitchens, they are not my first choice. I especially love darker-stained wood for its richness and warmth. But, I also find many types of marble and stone appealing, and either can be softened with area rugs. All of these elements combine to create a kitchen that not only will perform its function, but that also will be an inviting and comfortable space that you, your family, and friends can enjoy.

There is something timeless and classic about simple, white cabinets, selected over more elaborate models in this Hamptons kitchen that features an oversize island and multiple work areas.

A built-in window seat is a cozy and space-saving element in the casual family-dining area of this Hamptons kitchen. Along with several chairs, it offers plenty of seating around an oval pedestal table.

A kitchen is not just a place to prepare food; it is also a place to sit down to a lovely, family-style meal. Autumn is a wonderful time in the Hamptons to enjoy an elegant luncheon at a table set with whimsical gourd tureens holding a tasty pumpkin soup.

Custom walnut cabinetry echoes the curved walls of the kitchen in a contemporary-style
Los Angeles home. Isamu Noguchi goatskin lights hang like clouds above a classic Noguchi
table in the adjacent dining area. Framed photographic art and three flat-screen
televisions, which allow for multiple-channel viewing, are striking design elements.

White stainless-steel–trimmed cabinets in the kitchen-breakfast room of a Palm Beach town house were chosen to create a lighter impression in a space where limited natural light is available.

New York City kitchens are traditionally not very spacious, but a window in this high-rise midtown apartment assists in visually expanding the space, as does the clean, white cabinetry and mirrored backsplashes. A small area of the countertop in the efficiently organized space serves as a spot to pull up a stool and have morning coffee or an afternoon snack. Framed photographs are by Jeff Reese.

Beautiful Basics

I am an avid collector of many interesting things: French porcelains, books, black-and-white photographs, Parzinger and Laverne furniture, chinoiserie, and colorful Murano glass vessels from the 1930s and 1950s. Yet I believe that the most striking collection I have, which is a part of every home I occupy, is that of white dishes, tableware, and accessories.

I am not particular when it comes to the provenance of a piece. I find that high-quality white items from Crate & Barrel, Pottery Barn, or Pier One, which offer numerous choices that are within the budgets of most people, are just as lovely and probably more useful on a regular basis than precious and delicate antique porcelains. That is the beauty of these one-color pieces.

I love the purity associated with white, and its innate cleanliness and simplicity, especially when it is juxtaposed with the beautiful dark-wood finish of a table or display shelf. There is no need to worry about coordinating a tablescape when there is just one color from which to choose. The pieces can be of any style or period. In fact, the combination of antique and contemporary pieces makes more interesting visuals, at least to my eye. It is about the mixing, without having to worry about the matching. A traditional piece of English creamware, Spode, or unpainted Staffordshire, with somewhat elaborate detailing and texture, therefore can comfortably share the spotlight with the most utilitarian, undecorated charger of more recent vintage. Whenever I put white collections together for clients, encourage friends to amass their own sets of objects, or gather a variety of pieces together for display in my retail stores, I am always amazed at the reaction. There is something about the simplicity of one-color collections that pleases just about everyone.

A display of traditional and contemporary white tableware and other objects, of various textures and shapes, is always striking.

At Your Service

While interior designers are generally more focused on the front-of-house rooms, I look upon the creation of a home with an expanded point of view and hold the belief that no residence project can be considered complete without paying attention to the behind-the-scenes areas. The service rooms in a home—the pantry, garage, laundry room, storage rooms, and even basement—should not be neglected.

Organization is one of my priorities. A service room has to be properly equipped, orderly, and attractively designed. In fact, it is in these rooms that the lion's share of work in the house is done, often contributing to the overall efficiency of the household.

I think of these areas as extensions of the kitchen, where design and space planning is a top priority. The laundry room especially should be clean and bright, lit either naturally or with good artificial lighting. If you are spending any time there at all, consider making the room one in which you would want to be. Plenty of counter space is helpful and, if possible, there should be enough clear floor space for sorting baskets, hampers, clothing racks, and an ironing board. I also find it helpful to include a large stainless-steel utility sink, in which you can bathe the dog or arrange flowers.

Working areas should be designed with aesthetics in mind. This combination laundry room and mudroom in a Hamptons residence is a bright and cheerful space in which to accomplish many household chores. Whether doing a load of laundry or arranging flowers, the enjoyment factor is elevated by the design of the room. A French country table adds charm and is an unexpected addition.

In a Hamptons home, storage closets for tableware are set up in the kitchen to house the homeowner's extensive collection of antique china, crystal, and sterling-silver serving pieces for use in the dining room. Additional cabinetry has been installed in the garage for the storage of an eighty-piece service used for entertaining outdoors, along with the accessories that complement it.

The Greater Outdoors

Exterior Rooms and Gardens

Capturing a sense of glamour is certainly possible through the design of the outdoor areas surrounding a home. After all, design does not stop at the door. A distinct look should be clear as you approach a home; and it should continue from the entry through to the interior rooms, and out to the patio, veranda, terrace, pool area, and grounds beyond. To spend even a short portion of your day under the sun or starlight can be peaceful and relaxing.

Locations such as Southern California and South Florida are especially conducive to the indoor-outdoor lifestyle. Another destination that I enjoy is the East End of Long Island. The gardens in the Hamptons are unique and conducive to breezy, summertime, outdoor living. Here, I have created the house and garden that I love and cherish.

Designing a wonderful, comfortable exterior environment is not difficult. A beautifully manicured lawn, flowering shrubs, indigenous trees, and flowers are some of the ingredients that will make your time spent outdoors a pleasure. The first step to making your ideal garden is to envision how you and your guests will utilize the space. I make no secret of my aesthetic leanings, which are perhaps best described as "less is more." When it comes to the creation of exterior spaces, I apply the same design principles that I would apply indoors. On a patio, veranda, terrace, or around a pool, I begin by arranging multiple seating areas, establishing a look that is both uniform and comfortable.

The design of the outdoor furniture should reflect the style of the home. With a traditional house, I would use classic wicker furniture and a mixture of iron pieces—either new or antique. A sleek, modern residence requires more contemporary, clean-lined furniture and decorative elements. If appropriate, you may want to add an antique piece such as a jardiniere, sculpture, or other garden ornament for contrast. Seating, whether for open-air dining or lounging around, should be chosen for comfort, but, additionally, arranged so that prime views of the garden or the surrounding grounds can be taken in with ease. Any furniture selected should be weatherproof, even if it is placed on a covered porch, balcony, or terrace. There is an abundance of handsome outdoor pieces and decorative fabrics from which to choose that are readily available.

I love alfresco dining because it is always more relaxing and comfortable. The atmosphere is wonderfully casual. There is always room for one more guest at the table, and everything just seems more festive. While the way you organize an outdoor dining room should mirror the approach you take indoors, there is plenty of room for imagination and creativity. All of these elements combined make the outdoor experience more special and memorable.

For landscaping outdoor areas, I prefer a natural look that will be pleasing throughout the seasons. Of course, the garden, like the architecture and interior design of a residence, should be reflective of its particular location. I think of each outdoor area as a room unto itself, a background that brings enjoyment at every turn. When in a four-season place, such as the Hamptons, there is always something more special about a garden that has interest throughout the year. I am enchanted by the perpetual changes that occur in my own garden, and have chosen plantings carefully to provide a new experience as the seasons progress. In many ways, my preferences in garden design mirror those of my interior designs. I believe in keeping the look relatively simple and attractive.

Though recently built, this Hamptons residence was intended to appear as if it has been around for at least one hundred years. A lush lawn and foundation plantings of evergreens and perennials traditionally found in the area welcome visitors to the property.

Spring daisies and other perennials enliven a slope in a Hamptons
garden, where a series of outdoor "rooms" was conceived
to offer a range of visual experiences to those wandering through them.

Entertaining Outdoors

One of my greatest pleasures is hosting a cocktail, luncheon, or dinner party outside. Even if the guest list consists of just a few friends or family members, I delight in being able to savor fine food and drink in a more casual and relaxed fashion. A summer evening spent on the veranda of my Bridgehampton home has become one of my favorite forms of entertaining. Guests can meander through the garden and pool area and, both before and after the meal, gather in groups for conversation in the variety of sofas and chairs positioned expressly for that purpose. They dine at a table that is beautifully set for the service of a superbly prepared meal of fresh, often locally farmed vegetables, and delicious, simply grilled fish, fowl, or beef.

Proper lighting is essential when planning outdoor spaces that will be used for entertaining. Candlelight, supplemented by permanent fixtures or outdoor lamps that can be dimmed to appropriately soft levels, will enable you to set the right mood for your parties. For evening gatherings, you never want it to be too dark or too bright.

If you intend to invite a larger group, you must make certain, just as you would when entertaining a group indoors in the dining room, that there is plenty of room at each table and, if hiring staff to serve, that the space between the tables is ample enough for easy passage. At my house, there is a veranda that stretches across the south-facing facade. I designed it to comfortably accommodate seated parties of up to eighty people as well as a catering crew. There is convenient access to the kitchen and to the garage, where setups for the largest parties are usually placed. The cooking is done on grills just outside the kitchen. I also put a separate powder room in the garage for the convenience of catering staff, gardeners, and other service people. It is this attention to detail that contributes to a successful and seamlessly executed alfresco event.

Right: The Hamptons house was designed to include a generously scaled veranda, which serves as an open-air living room. Conducive to outdoor living, it offers plenty of space for relaxation and dining. *Following page:* The spacious, columned veranda was planned as a place to live outdoors in the summer months as well as to entertain.

Like any indoor gathering space, the Hamptons veranda is organized with several seating groups. Weatherproof furnishings and fabrics are essential when outfitting an outdoor "room."

Classically modern
Richard Schultz outdoor
furniture, including
chaises and a dining
table and chairs,
installed year-round
on the rooftop terrace
of a Los Angeles home,
are in keeping with
the contemporary
look of the residence's
architecture.

Above: An antique Balinese temple structure offers a shady retreat in a Hamptons garden
setting. *Right:* The small hedged-in and well-manicured yard behind a midtown Palm Beach
town house was improved by both the addition of a mosaic wall fountain built on one side
of the refurbished pool and the extension of the deck to the perimeter of the formerly
uninviting backyard. The Richard Schultz dining table and chairs allow for impromptu poolside
luncheons and intimate dinner parties. *Following pages:* The terrain behind the Hamptons
house called out for a terraced garden, with natural stone steps linking the several levels
below, including the pool area, where Richard Schultz chaises and tables are positioned
under umbrellas. The blue-and-white color scheme chosen for a Hamptons residence extends
to the covered terrace and pool deck, arranged for outdoor entertaining and dining.

Afterword

I have worked long and hard to establish not only a company that provides furniture, lighting, fabrics, and accessories, but also what I like to think of as a recognizable design aesthetic that combines both the practical and the beautiful. My success in the interior design industry has allowed me to have exposure to so many wonderful things, brilliant people, and exciting, often exotic places. These experiences have definitely affected my sensibility and sense of adventure in terms of my design outlook. I still value simplicity over all, no matter whether in design, fashion, or cuisine.

In setting up homes and offices for family and for clients, I have been challenged to encourage individuality while sharing more than a little of what I consider to be glamorous and also necessary—the elements and techniques that I have picked up or instinctively added to my repertoire over the years.

I know that not everyone is as confident or comfortable about making decisions about decorating as I am, but hopefully what I have presented and discussed in the previous pages will assist or inspire you to make your home a more pleasant and refined place to live. My life is not solely focused on design. I believe that in order to have a fulfilling life, one must give something back in whatever way possible. Since losing my beloved mother to Alzheimer's six years ago, I have made it my goal to devote as much of my life and resources as possible to organizations such as the Alzheimer's Drug Discovery Foundation, which is dedicated to finding a cure for this dreaded disease. And, realizing how fortunate I am to have my two wonderful girls, Coco and Lily, I am also an advocate for homeless and forgotten animals. Helping others makes the world a more beautiful place.

Acknowledgments

When you design an interior, a piece of furniture, or a fabric, it is never a solo effort. There are many people involved in creating the final result. So is the case with a book, which begins with a simple idea that is developed over time by a team whose members make individual and valuable contributions. This book probably never would have come to fruition had Beth Daugherty of Potterton Books not first proposed it. Beth said, "Nancy, why don't you write a book?" The thought had never occurred to me. Her suggestion started the wheels in motion.

Victoria Montana has contributed her talent and boundless energy throughout the years, organizing photographic shoots across the country. Her perseverance made the visuals happen. Douglas Johnson has operated and managed my factory, and given me unwavering support and advice for more than twenty years. Andrew Gerhard taught me about the importance of great architecture. Dennis Hunt and Suzy Garfield, my right and left arms, are my toughest editors. Designer Doug Turshen's exacting eye made everything look beautiful in print. Sandy Gilbert, my patient and painstaking editor, took all the bits and pieces and formulated the vision. Robert Janjigian made the writing process enjoyable, and interjected humor and insight.

My staff—Dawn Hanley, Tracie Jahn—and Christina Juarez, are deserving of my heartfelt thanks, as are the many talented photographers whose work appears in these pages.

Last, but certainly not least, I wish to express my deepest gratitude to Mark Locks, who has encouraged and counseled me for the past five years, through all the trials and the triumphs.

First published in the United States of America in 2009
by Rizzoli International Publications, Inc.
300 Park Avenue South
New York, New York 10010
www.rizzoliusa.com

2009 2010 2011 2012 / 10 9 8 7 6 5 4 3 2 1

Printed in China

ISBN 13: 978-0-8478-3340-5

Library of Congress Control Number: 2009928418

Project Editor: Sandra Gilbert
Art Direction: Doug Turshen

Photography Credits

The following photographers have been instrumental in making this book possible. I am also extremely grateful to Victor Boghossian for all of his efforts in the photography editing and retouching process.

Carter Berg: pages 80, 139

Miguel Flores-Vianna: pages 9, 34, 35, 94, 123, 188

Tria Giovan: page 42

David Glomb: pages 58, 60, 62, 63

Michael Grimm: page 198

Mick Hales: pages 3, 163, 177, 186, 212, 213, 216, 218

Ken Hayden: pages 13, 14, 15, 16, 17, 18, 19, 20, 21, 23, 38, 39, 44, 46, 47, 48, 50, 51, 54, 56, 65, 66, 68, 70, 71, 72, 73, 74, 76, 78, 90, 92, 95, 99, 100, 101, 103, 112, 113, 114, 115, 119, 120, 122, 124, 125, 126, 129, 130, 131, 135, 136, 140, 141, 145, 146, 148, 149, 150, 152, 154, 156, 157, 158, 160, 164, 168, 170, 171, 172, 178, 179, 180, 185, 190, 191,192, 194, 197, 200, 201, 206, 207, 209, 210, 214, 217, 223

Thomas Loof: pages 36, 40, 41, 87, 128, 181

Peter Margonelli: pages 32, 88, 89

Marni Steel (courtesy *Veranda* magazine): pages 108, 110, 111

Andy Strauss: pages 24–25, 82–83, 104–105, 132, 134, 174–175

Eric Striffler: page 205

Peter Vitale (courtesy *Veranda* magazine): pages 5, 29, 30, 52, 53, 96, 98, 107, 166